GW00367510

# IMAGES OF
# BATH
### World Heritage City

## Photographed by John Curtis

## SALMON

# INTRODUCTION

Renowned throughout the world as one of Britain's most beautiful cities, historic Bath is set on the River Avon, among the rolling hills of North Somerset. Although it is celebrated as the best-preserved Georgian city in the country, the rich and fascinating history of this elegant city reaches far back to Roman times and beyond.

Legend has it that Bath's famous hotsprings were discovered in 850 BC, when the fabled Prince Bladud contracted leprosy, was banished from court to the Avon Valley and became a swineherd at Swainswick. He noticed that the pigs in his care, after wallowing in the warm muddy marshes, seemed to be completely cured of their skin conditions. On closer inspection of the marshes, he discovered that they were fed by an abundant hot spring and, after immersing himself in the mud, his leprosy miraculously disappeared. When he was welcomed back into society and later became king, Bladud showed his appreciation by building a bath around the restorative spring, and thus the beginnings of the city of Bath were born.

In the Iron Age, the Celtic goddess Sul was worshipped as the guardian to the gateway of the Underworld, and the Celts guarded this sacred site where water bubbled from the ground, with five hillforts which dominated the hot spring from the surrounding hilltops.

After the Roman invasion, the city became known as Aquae Sulis, or Sul's Waters. Intrigued by the steaming hot springs, the

*Bath from Beechen Cliff*

Romans drained the marsh and contained the waters, constructing Britain's first health spa and a temple, which they dedicated to Sulis Minerva, a blend of the Celtic goddess Sul with their own goddess Minerva. They built a reservoir to control the flow of waters, lining it with lead mined from the Mendip Hills, and the overflow can still be seen today tumbling through a Roman arch. When the Romans left Britain in AD 410, the site returned to its original marshy state and, as masonry crumbled, it sank into the marsh. The Great Bath stayed hidden for centuries, later being discovered by the Victorians, but the hot spring still flowed and a healing centre was run by monks around its remains.

During the 18th century, Bath became popular once again as a health resort, after the city's leading physician, Dr. William Oliver, encouraged bathing in the thermal springs as a remedy for gout, rheumatism and a plethora of other ailments. Over a period of 100 years, Bath's population grew from around 2,000 to nearly 30,000 citizens. The city became a lively and fashionable social centre, attracting many visitors, under the influence of socialite and inveterate gambler Beau Nash, a dandy who was intent on transforming Bath into a city of pleasure.

In 1727, a trench was dug to lay sewers, unearthing the gilded bronze head of Minerva, but it was another sixty years before the splendid Roman temple was discovered.

Much of the magnificent city we see today is due to the considerable brilliance, vision and artistry of architects John Wood and his son of the same name, and entrepreneur and quarry owner Ralph Allen, who provided the distinctive pale golden Bath stone. A city of supreme beauty and elegance was designed, with sweeping crescents, elegant squares, and handsome parks and public buildings. Bath is now a World Heritage City, considered by many to be one of the loveliest in the world.

*Roman Baths, the Great Bath*

## Roman Baths Museum

This fearsome Gorgon's head, thought to be the Medusa, with writhing snakes for hair, originally glared down from its elevated position on the pediment above four immense columns at the entrance to the temple. It is now displayed with the remains of the pediment in the Roman Baths Museum.

## Spring Overflow

Much of the original Roman plumbing and drainage is still in place, bearing testament to the Romans' highly-developed engineering skills, and surplus water from the sacred spring is emptied into the River Avon via this superb overflow system. Stained red by the iron content of the water, the spring overflow still serves the purpose for which it was designed.

### The King's Bath

Overlooked by a statue of Bladud, the magnificent King's Bath was built in the 12th century, and continued in its capacity as a place for therapeutic bathing until the middle of the 20th century. Built on the site of the ancient sacred spring reservoir, it was constructed using original Roman stones.

### Head of Minerva, The Roman Baths Museum

At the start of the 19th century, the entire Roman baths complex was unearthed, and the remains and other artefacts are now displayed in the Roman Baths Museum. One of its best-known exhibits is the beautiful gilded bronze head of the statue of the Roman goddess, Minerva, which was found by workmen in 1727.

## The Pump Room

Situated above the Roman reservoir and overlooking the King's Bath, the elegant Pump Room, designed by Thomas Baldwin, was where Beau Nash presided as Master of Ceremonies in the 18th century. It became the hub of Bath's social life, and fashionable Georgian society flocked to this sumptuous room in order to drink the curative waters from the spring, and socialise at elaborate banquets, dances and breakfasts.

## The King's Spring

The lavish Pump Room has Corinthian columns, an impressive chandelier and a Greek inscription above the entrance, proclaiming 'Water is Best'. The hot spa water, which contains 43 minerals and elements, can still be tasted here. It is dispensed from this delightful spa water fountain, called the King's Spring, and is at a constant temperature of 46°C.

### Bath Abbey and the Abbey Churchyard

Standing in the heart of the city, next to the Pump Rooms, Bath Abbey was built on the site of a vast old cathedral, where Edgar was crowned the first King of England in 973. The abbey was started in 1499, by Bishop Oliver King, as a result of his interpretation of a dream he had, in which angels ascended and descended ladders between heaven and earth, and voices proclaimed, "Let an olive establish the crown and a king restore the church". In front of the abbey, the pedestrianised Abbey Churchyard is lined with cafés and shops, and is an ideal spot to watch the various street entertainers, taking in the glorious splendour of the surrounding architecture.

## Bath Abbey Interior

Often referred to as the 'Lantern of the West', because it has more window than wall, Bath Abbey has a breathtaking 52 windows, including the spectacular east windows which depict numerous scenes in the life of Christ. The most impressive architectural feature of the abbey's Perpendicular-style interior is the glorious stone-carved, fan-vaulted ceiling, designed by Robert and William Vertue in the 16th century, and fully completed in the 19th century by George Gilbert Scott.

## Alkmaar Garden, Orange Grove

Outside the abbey is Orange Grove, named after a visit by William of Orange in 1734, and the circular Alkmaar Garden, housing an attractive obelisk, which takes its name from a Dutch town, one of four towns twinned with the city.

## The Guildhall

Dating from 1776, the splendid Guildhall was built by Thomas Baldwin to designs by Thomas Warr Atwood, and was originally intended for use as the town hall. Surmounting the pediment of the building is a handsome lead statue of the Scales of Justice, and intricate carved friezes are featured on the exterior walls.

## Banqueting Room, The Guildhall

Adorned with elegant chandeliers and royal portraits by Joshua Reynolds, the lavish Banqueting Room is the largest room in the Guildhall. One of the most outstanding interiors in Bath, the building was once favoured by the wealthy traders of Bath, who were excluded from the Assembly Rooms. It is a popular venue for weddings and serves as the city's register office.

## Parade Gardens

Providing a tranquil retreat near the abbey, in the bustling heart of the city, Parade Gardens is a delightful public park, known for its outstanding floral bedding displays. Situated beside the River Avon, the park overlooks magnificent 18th century Pulteney Bridge and the weir. Concerts are performed regularly throughout the summer months in the bandstand, and deckchairs are available.

## The Fountain, Terrace Walk

Opposite Parade Gardens, this charming fountain stands on Terrace Walk. It was moved here from its original position in Stall Street, where it was once used as a free public drinking fountain, from which people could drink the hot mineral water from Bath's natural springs.

## Sally Lunn's House
The oldest house in the city, Sally Lunn's house, situated in North Parade Passage, has a 17th century façade, but some of the foundations date back to the 12th century. Famous for bringing the French recipe for brioche to England, when as a Huguenot refugee she came to work in the bakery, Sally Lunn's buns became so popular that her house became a fashionable place for people to meet, and the buns became known as Bath buns.

## Abbey Green
This tranquil little refuge, once the site of a 17th century bowling green, nestles behind the Roman baths and the abbey, providing an oasis of calm in the busy city. The plane tree in the centre of Abbey Green is more than 200 years old, and the Crystal Palace pub, once called The Three Tunns, is where Lord Nelson recuperated from injuries sustained in the Battle of the Nile in 1798.

## The Cross Bath, Bath Street

Connecting the main Roman Baths and Pump Room to the beautiful building of the Cross Bath, is the elegantly colonnaded Bath Street. It was built by Thomas Baldwin, in 1791, to provide cover for bathers moving between the two sites. The Cross Bath, which is at the western end of the street, stands above its own spring, on the sacred site where the Celts worshipped their goddess, Sul.

## Bath Street

Wherever you turn in the captivating, richly historical city of Bath, there are statues, sculptures and figurines, works of art and treasures from a bygone era. These figures in the window of a building in attractive 18th century Bath Street may originally have been from the old Guildhall or the City Gate.

**Minerva Bath, Thermae Bath Spa**
Named after the Roman goddess, the largest of the thermal baths at the stylish new spa complex is the gracefully curving Minerva Bath, which has a whirlpool, massage jets and a swirling 'lazy river'. There are also several aroma steam rooms and an open-air rooftop pool, from where there are spectacular views of the city and surrounding hills.

**Hot Bath, Thermae Bath Spa**
A long history of public bathing ended in Bath in 1978, after the closure of the municipal baths in Beau Street. In 2006, the Thermae Bath Spa opened, giving bathers access once more to the mineral-rich waters once enjoyed by the Celts and the Romans. This luxurious spa offers both indoor and outdoor bathing.

## Old Bond Street

Exuding charming Regency ambience, the delightful, pedestrianised Old Bond Street has a range of interesting little shops and cafés. From here the grand old building of the Royal Mineral Water Hospital is visible. Like much of the architecture in Bath, it was designed by John Wood, using the famous Bath stone supplied by quarry owner Ralph Allen. The hospital is known as The Royal National Hospital for Rheumatic Diseases.

## Theatre Royal

Situated in Sawclose, the Theatre Royal is sandwiched between two houses that were both lived in by Beau Nash. There has been a Theatre Royal in Bath since 1768, although the one on this site dates from 1805. Considered to be one of the most beautiful theatres in the country, the Theatre Royal is host to various festivals throughout the year, including the renowned Bath Shakespeare Festival.

**Beaufort Square**

Situated at what is now the rear of the splendid Theatre Royal, elegant and charming Beaufort Square was laid out by architect John Strahan in 1730, and was once the site of the main entrance to the theatre. In the centre is a peaceful communal garden, with wrought iron railings enclosing a small rectangular lawn.

**Queen Square**

Celebrated architect John Wood's first large project, Queen Square, was begun in 1729. Strongly influenced by Italian architect Palladio's use of classical styles, Wood modelled the square on an Italian piazza. The imposing obelisk in the centre commemorates a visit to the city by Frederick, Prince of Wales.

## The Circus

Consisting of three splendid crescents arranged in a tight circle of three-storey houses, with a carved frieze running around the entire circle, The Circus was the brainchild of John Wood the Elder. He died before the fulfillment of his design, which was inspired by Rome's Colosseum, but it was completed by his son.

## Gay Street

Leading from The Circus to graceful Queen Square, is Gay Street, another handsome street designed by John Wood the Elder. It was once the home of the writer Jane Austen, who lived at No. 25, and there is a museum dedicated to her at No. 40. The three-storey houses here, some with Ionic columns, have mansard roofs.

### Royal Victoria Park

Overlooked by the spectacular Royal Crescent, spacious Royal Victoria Park, laid out by city architect, Edward Davis, is one of the many enchanting parks and gardens for which Bath is famous. It includes the Botanical Gardens and a bandstand. This mid-19th century gate post with a lion is one of a pair marking the gates to Royal Avenue from Queen's Parade.

### The Victoria Column, Royal Victoria Park

Opened in 1830, Royal Victoria Park was named after the young Princess Victoria, who was visiting Bath at the time. An obelisk, designed by G.P. Manners, was erected in honour of the princess's 18th birthday. During her stay here as a child, Victoria felt unhappy, and developed a life-long dislike of the city of Bath, to which she never returned.

**Botanical Garden, Royal Victoria Park**
The exquisite Royal Victoria Horticultural and Botanical Garden was formed in Royal Victoria Park in 1839. This beautiful nine-acre garden includes a rock garden, glorious herbaceous borders and sculptures and, behind these delightfully blossoming trees stands a replica of the Roman Temple of Minerva.

**Royal Crescent**
John Wood the Younger's spectacular Royal Crescent took seven years to construct and was completed in 1774. A semi-elliptical terrace of graceful houses, decorated with 114 Ionic columns, this crescent sits above a sweeping lawn, and provides incomparable views over the city of Bath.

## Somerset Place

Completed in the 1820s, Somerset Place was designed by architect John Eveleigh. The houses in this Grade I listed crescent feature doorways with architraves on rusticated blocks, carved keystones, consoles and entablatures. There is a curved, six-bay segmental broken pediment at the centre of the façade, decorated with large discs and swags.

## Cavendish Crescent, Cavendish Lodge and Lansdown Crescent

Blending superbly with its magnificent Georgian surroundings, Cavendish Lodge is a recent development of 20 apartments, built in 1997. Overlooking the city, it is situated on Cavendish Road, below John Palmer's famous Lansdown Crescent, and John Pinch's Cavendish Crescent.

## Lansdown Crescent

Distinguished, Grade I listed Lansdown Crescent was built between 1789 and 1793 by a variety of builders, though it was designed by John Palmer. From its lofty position on Lansdown Hill, there are far-reaching views over the city of Bath. The crescent was the home of the well-known, eccentric English author, enthusiastic art collector and MP for Wells, William Beckford, who lived at Nos. 19 and 20.

## Camden Crescent

Named after the Marquis of Camden, Recorder of Bath from 1759–61, Camden Crescent was built by John Eveleigh in 1788. The crescent suffered a landslide in 1889, which destroyed nine of the houses on the east side, where Hedgemead Park was later laid out. As a result, the central pediment which bears the Marquis of Camden's coat of arms is no longer in the centre.

## Belmont, Lansdown Road

Situated on the east side of Lansdown Road, Belmont is a handsome terrace of houses and a fine example of the mellow, pale honey-coloured Bath stone used in so much of the architecture in the city. Thought to be the work of city architect Thomas Atwood, John Wood the Younger's rival, the houses were built between 1770 and 1773, and it is believed that they interfered with some of Wood's own architectural ambitions.

## Tea Room, Assembly Rooms

Set in the heart of the city, the magnificent Assembly Rooms were designed by John Wood the Younger in 1769. Fashionable Georgian society gathered here to take tea or play cards, and for dances, functions and general socialising. These superb rooms include the beautiful pillared Tea Room, which has three Georgian chandeliers and is available to hire for weddings and functions.

## Ballroom, Assembly Rooms

The highest echelons of Bath's Georgian society flocked to dine and dance in the lavish surroundings of the Assembly Rooms. With its beautiful powder-blue walls, elaborate cornicing and five sparkling chandeliers, the opulent ballroom is the largest Georgian interior in the city. Fully restored to their original splendour, the Assembly Rooms also house an outstanding Fashion Museum.

## Church of St. Swithin, Walcot

There has been a church on this site at Walcot since AD 971, but the present church was designed by John Palmer, who built Lansdown Crescent. It was consecrated in 1777, extended in 1788, and a classical spire was added in 1790. Writer Jane Austen's father, the Rev George Austen, was married to Cassandra Leigh at St. Swithin's, and, in 1805, he was also buried here.

### The Paragon

Designed in 1768 by Thomas Warr Atwood, and finished by John Palmer, The Paragon terrace is situated near the city centre, on one of Bath's best-known streets, Roman Road. Presenting a typical view of Bath's serene appeal and Georgian architectural splendour, these black iron railings contrast beautifully with the pale golden Bath stone of the buildings. Although the houses look out over a busy road, the rear windows enjoy fine views of the River Avon and the delightful surrounding countryside.

### The Building of Bath Museum

Housed in the Countess of Huntingdon's 18th century Chapel, the Building of Bath Museum opened in 1992. Exhibits and artefacts give an insight into the Georgian way of life and tell the story of how the Georgian city of Bath was developed, designed and built.

## Pulteney Bridge

Based on the Ponte Vecchio in Florence, with shops on either side, majestic Pulteney Bridge was completed in 1774 and is the only example of Robert Adam's work in Bath. Spanning the River Avon, this three-arched bridge was commissioned by wealthy landowner William Pulteney, who intended to build a suburb of Bath on the opposite side of the river.

## Trompe l'Oeil on Grove Street

On the corner where Pulteney Bridge meets the junction of Grove Street and Argyle Street, this skillfully executed Trompe l'Oeil on the first floor, above what is now a restaurant, depicts a man in his library reading a book. The faded writing on the exterior wall above the window suggests this was once a book shop and lending library.

**Sydney Place, Jane Austen's House**
Famously the home of Jane Austen for most of
her time as resident of Bath, 4 Sydney Place
was built around 1800. There is a small plaque
outside No 4, to commemorate the celebrated
author's time here. Originally from Hampshire
and a lover of the countryside, she apparently
fainted on being told by her parents of their
intention to move to the city of Bath, but it
proved to be a valuable resource for her writing.

**Laura Place and Great Pulteney Street**
Between Pulteney Bridge and Great Pulteney
Street, Laura Place has a delightful fountain,
and was built by Thomas Baldwin and John
Eveleigh, and completed in 1794. The widest
and grandest thoroughfare in Bath, Great
Pulteney Street's former residents include royal
mistress Maria Fitzherbert and Nelson's
mistress Lady Hamilton.

## Holburne Museum

Set in the glorious surroundings of Sydney Pleasure Gardens, the Holburne Museum of Art, built by Charles Harcourt Masters in 1796, was originally designed as the Sydney Hotel. After several changes of use, the building was converted in the early 20th century to become the home of Holburne Museum, housing Sir William Holburne's distinguished art collection.

## Sydney Gardens

The oldest park in Bath, charming Sydney Gardens, also planned and laid out by Charles Harcourt Masters, opened in 1795. The gardens became a popular place for fashionable society to meet for breakfasts, galas and evening promenades, and were much frequented by Jane Austen when she lived nearby, at Sydney Place.

### Kennet and Avon Canal and Cleveland House

The Kennet and Avon Canal was laid through Sydney Gardens in 1810 and, with its ornamental foot bridges and tunnels designed by John Rennie, it added to the attractions of the park. Running underneath the former headquarters of the Kennet and Avon Canal Company, Cleveland House, is the 173-feet-long Cleveland Tunnel. There is a delightful towpath walk from the park to Bath railway station.

### Kennet and Avon Canal, Widcombe

The Kennet and Avon Canal leaves the River Avon at Bath and, at Widcombe, there is a flight of six locks, which raises the level of the waterway by 65 feet. The canal fell into disuse in the late 19th century and was restored in the later part of the 20th century. Today, it is a popular beauty spot and narrowboat trips can be taken from the Widcombe Top Lock.

**River Avon**
Reflected in the waters of the beautiful River Avon, even these former industrial buildings have a certain grace and charm, and serve as a reminder of the city's heritage and past importance as an inland commercial port. Also known as the Lower Avon or the Bristol Avon, the river loops around the World Heritage city.

**City from Abbey View Gardens**
Seen here from Abbey View Gardens, Bath is set against a backdrop of ancient hill country. Encircled by seven hills, the city nestles in a sheltered valley, like an amphitheatre. Its numerous crescents and terraces ascend the surrounding slopes in tiers, each offering far-reaching views over the city below.

### Sham Castle

Built in 1762 by Ralph Allen's master mason, Richard James, this eye-catching folly in the Bathampton area was intended to make the view more interesting from Ralph Allen's town house in the city where he made his fortune. Today, this is a popular spot for walks and picnics and provides superb views over the city.

### Prior Park Landscape Garden

Built for entrepreneur and philanthropist Ralph Allen, sumptuous Prior Park is a spectacular Palladian mansion set on the slopes of Combe Down. The splendid 18th century landscape garden offers extensive views over the city, and contains three lakes and one of the only four Palladian bridges of this style in the world.

## Claverton Manor

East of Bath, in the village of Claverton, Claverton Manor was designed by Jeffry Wyatville and is set in extensive grounds. Home of the American Museum in Britain, this Grade I listed mansion boasts an enchanting garden with an arboretum devoted to American trees and shrubs, and herb and vegetable gardens. There is also the Mount Vernon Garden, a replica of George Washington's flower garden in Virginia. Set high on the hill, the house and grounds provide magnificent views over the River Avon and the Limpley Stoke Valley.

## Widcombe Manor

Standing beside 15th century St. Thomas à Becket Church, in tranquil Widcombe, Widcombe Manor was originally built in 1656. Writer Henry Fielding stayed at the lodge here, while working on the famous novel *Tom Jones*.

**Sir Bevil Grenville's Monument**
Positioned on Lansdown Hill, this grand monument was erected in 1720, to commemorate the bravery of Sir Bevil Grenville, who commanded a Royalist troop of Cornish soldiers at the Battle of Lansdown, in 1643. Now a Scheduled Ancient Monument, it marks the spot where he was mortally wounded.

**Kennet and Avon Canal, Bathampton**
Two miles east of the city, the Kennet and Avon Canal cuts through the little village of Bathampton. This scenic canal is popular with boating enthusiasts, whose boats can be moored beside The George. This 12th century pub was once a monastery and still retains its original priests' hole which runs across to the church.

## Bath Racecourse

Situated on Lansdown Hill, overlooking the city, Bath Racecourse is one of the highest in the country. As well as the usual horseracing fixtures, the course has hosted the Ham National, a pig racing event where the contestants have amusing racing-related names such as Desert Porchid. Notable races at Bath include the Lansdown and Dick Hern Fillies' Stakes.

## William Beckford's Tomb and Tower

Commissioned by author, traveller and distinguished art collector William Beckford, this neo-classical tower was completed in 1827. Designed by Henry Goodridge, Beckford's Tower, on Lansdown Hill, offers superb views over surrounding countryside. Beckford died in 1844 and his marble tomb is in Lansdown Cemetery.

# Roman Baths, The Great Bath

Standing at the heart of the Roman Baths and overlooked by the Abbey is the impressive Great Bath, which was unearthed by the Victorians in the 1880s. Lined with thick sheets of lead and just over five feet deep, with steps leading down on all sides, this grand pool was fed by the sacred hot spring, and provided ideal conditions for the luxury of swimming in warm water.

Published in Great Britain by J. Salmon Ltd., Sevenoaks, Kent TN13 1BB. Telephone 01732 452381.
Email enquiries@jsalmon.co.uk

Design by John Curtis.

With thanks to Bath & North East Somerset Council, Bath Abbey, The National Trust and the Thermae Bath Spa.

Photographs © John Curtis except on pages 5, 6, 7, 8, 9, 10, 11, 17, 41, 42, 64 © John Curtis/ Bath & North East Somerset Council.

ISBN 978-1-84640-295-1

Printed in China.

Title page photograph: Royal Crescent
Front cover photograph: Royal Victoria Park
Back cover photograph: Thermae Bath Spa – Rooftop Pool
First Edition 2011

Salmon Books

# ENGLISH IMAGES SERIES

Photography by John Curtis

*Titles available in this series*